a

[handwritten: nonfiction book so far, and I really expect to only write novels after this.]

CHIPS OF

GRANITE

[signature: Dennis Lanning]

Dennis Lanning

Chips of Granite
Copyright © 2018 by Dennis Lanning

Dedication

In appreciation for their great love, I dedicate this book to the congregation of Marshallville United Methodist Church, and to their music director, who also happens to be my wife.

Table of Contents

Preface

God is still working on me. In fact, God is still working on all of us.

 I think of God as a sculptor, and you and I are like large pieces of granite. God knows the masterpieces we can become, but chips will have to be removed by hammer and chisel to reveal the image of beauty He knows is inside.

 Some changes we need are small, while some are dramatic. The short essays that I've written for my website, dennislanning.com, over the last few years are a chronicle of the work God has been doing on me. I pray that each short article in this book will also bring you closer to being what God envisions you to be.

 Chip away, Lord. The rubble of a hundred and one chips on the floor means more of Your masterpiece is now visible.

Chapter One: Time Management

As far as I can tell, God does not wear a watch. No one who has ever claimed to have seen God said He had a watch. God just does things at the appropriate time. We are not meant to be slaves to time.

Looking Ahead

Life is like an ever-flowing stream--- ever hear that? We live most of our lives in a routine or pattern, and nothing much is remarkable. It's like a flowing stream, and we just float along in the current. Where are we going? Well, there is childhood, adolescence, adulthood, middle age, old age, and then death.

Good grief! I want my life to be more exciting than that, don't you? We've got to look ahead and set a goal, and then *go for it!*

But there's no time to think about tomorrow. Today takes all the effort we can spare.

Actually, living life in an attitude of leaning forward takes very little more effort than living for today. But it sure is more fun, concentrating on what might be, what could be, what is to come, rather than reacting to what is being done to us right now.

So look ahead. Set a goal. Ask God what He would have you be, then set your eyes on things to come.

It just might put a smile on your face.

*****

Over-Listed

Mondays can be tough. Monday, for me, always starts with a list. What do I need to get done this week?

Every Monday, it's obvious that I have too much on my plate. I'm trying to do too much. I cannot possibly get it all done.

One option I've tried is to only list those things I need to get done immediately, like this morning, or maybe just list the minimum for today. The problem with that is I tend to forget tasks I don't write down. Then, when I've finished and crossed off my list the few things listed, I have to try to remember what I purposely didn't write down earlier. That seems like a waste of time.

Of course, if I list everything I need to do, it is a bit discouraging. That leads to slow progress, or just taking an extended break.

The best solution I've found, when I remember it, is from Psalm 46:10, "Be still, and know that I am God." Actually, the rest of the Psalm is necessary, too, reminding me that God's strength is a whole lot more than my own. Since I'm not God, He also has a better perspective. Maybe God never intended for me to complete everything I wrote on my 'to do' list.

God's list for what I need to get done probably looks very different from mine.

*****

Vacation, Rest, Sabbath

I guess we all need to be rejuvenated regularly. We need new life, and we go about it in different ways.

Vacation is meant to be a cure for being stuck in a rut and tired. Being away from our regular employment and routine can give a new perspective. Vacation often means going away to a different location; sometimes that has the accompanying effect of tiring us physically. That eclipses our rejuvenation.

Rejuvenation is often interwoven with physical rest. When we're tired from a heavy load, sleep and naps and just doing nothing can help us bounce back. I'm afraid that's only a partial, narrow rejuvenation.

The kind of rejuvenation I seek out is more than physical. If I'm well-rested, I don't always have energy! I need to get plugged in better to a power source that can give me continual life. Does that sound like an advertisement for a candy bar or energy drink? What I need is sabbath.

Somehow people got the idea that sabbath has to do with getting physically rested. They point to the establishment of a sabbath day, back in Genesis 2. God created everything in six days, and on the seventh day he rested. Was God so physically drained that he needed a day off to get his strength back?

The sabbath I need, and what I see promoted in the Bible, is a time of taking stock, a time to recenter ourselves on God. If I can get that, I can make it through another week in good fashion.

Remember the Sabbath, one of God's greatest gifts.

*****

Catching a Moving Train

It's my first day back at work, after a week off. It's hard to know where to start.

Everything wants to be the first task I tackle! It all needs to be done right away, but I'm not ready to move at top speed yet.

Life is like a moving train today. By this afternoon I'll match your speed and be back on the train. You don't need to wait for me.

A friend at seminary taught me the trick to walking with a full cup of coffee, and I think it applies here. To keep from spilling the coffee, you don't look at the cup, but instead focus on something that is not moving, like the corner of a window or a door post.

Today, I'm not going to focus on all the work I've got to get done this week. Most of the tasks are a moving target, without a particular time they have to be accomplished, and flexible as to size and shape. I'm going to focus on God's love for me, constant through time. It's how I'll get back on track.

"Trust in the Lord with all your heart, and lean not on your own understanding. In all your ways acknowledge him, and he will direct your paths." Proverbs 3:5-6

*****

Packing for Tomorrow

"So do not worry about tomorrow, for tomorrow will bring worries of its own. Today's trouble is enough for today." Matthew 6:34

I've never had a grandchild before. Our first is due in less than five weeks. Of course, that means she could arrive any time. My son and wife already have their bags packed for that thrilling trip to the hospital.

We want to be there, too. It'll be a three-hour drive, so we want to be able to get in the car at short notice. It's time for us to pack our bags, too.

It would sure be easier if we knew exactly what day we would need to go. I've been trying to stay a little ahead on my work, and I've got a great substitute to handle church services for me at a moment's notice. There's the matter of making sure I have a dog sitter, and keeping plenty of gas in the car, not leaving any bills unpaid, and just a lot of little details.

Thinking about that upcoming 'tomorrow' is stealing time from today! I try to keep focused on the main fact: The Lord will be in my tomorrows just as much as right now.

"And remember, I am with you always, to the end of the age." Matthew 28:20
*****

Tomorrow Can't Wait

I've got a vacation coming up. You'd think it was tomorrow.

Last week, or even a couple of days ago, I didn't really need a vacation, but now I do. It's a mental thing, I guess, but the closer a vacation comes, the more I need it. Ordinary chores seem so hard, knowing that vacation is just around the corner. Bigger chores seem huge: "I'd better not start on that yet. Vacation is coming."

All those little things that are part of everyday living, like cooking, cleaning, keeping up the yard become part of a countdown. "In three more days, I won't have to wash dishes for a week. In three days, I can stop setting the alarm clock every morning. In three more days, I can stop shaving for a week, if I want to."

With vacation looming, it can be hard to get things done. It's exactly the same as wasting time worrying. Tomorrow is

12

stealing from today, and all the fullness of living right now.

I guess that's what Jesus was talking about when he said, "Don't worry about tomorrow. Tomorrow will have enough worries of its own."

Somebody told me that Forest Gump was once asked to name two days of the week that begin with the letter "T." Do you know the answer? Forest said, "Today and tomorrow."

Today and tomorrow are not the same. Live today fully; tomorrow will get here soon enough.

*****

Messy Desk

One idea that time-management experts don't seem to agree on is a clean desk. Does it pay to have your work area tidy?

If your desk is not straight, it could be because you're not focused on your main objectives. You try to do too many things at once. They say, "If you don't know which way you're going, any path will get you there." An orderly work area indicates, perhaps, an orderly method of doing work. Things don't get out of hand.

However, it can also be said that a person can spend too much time keeping their desk straight. A little messiness might allow a little more time, to get a little more done. They say, "If you want something done, ask a busy person to do it."

Now, if it were possible, the best of both worlds would be to have an orderly, focused mind, knowing what your goals are at all times, with a desk that 'just looks messy.' Actually, you know where everything is in your work area, and it doesn't really matter that an outsider can't comprehend that.

Stay focused in your work for our Lord, and don't mind the little things that don't get done when others think they should.

*****

The Other Side of the Leaf

Some new years are easier than others, in that I can immediately start writing the date correctly. I remember that writing "2015" never was a problem that year, except that twice I put the date as 2007. (Was that one of my better years?)

This year just feels like one of those odd years that will give me difficulty writing the correct year on things. It just seems a strange number. It just doesn't have a comfortable sound to it. Oh, well.

My new year's resolutions have also given me more trouble. It's always great to 'turn over a new leaf.', but all these leaves have been turned over before! I've got to lose weight again. I've got to do a better job of keeping up with my calendar, again. I'm still trying to break the habit of starting to read and not finishing a nonfiction book. I listed twelve resolutions this year, and very few of them are new.

So I'll turn leaves over again this year. If you don't think you can change, it takes a chunk out of your character. You've got to be willing to make changes, and you've got to have hope that life can get better.

"Now faith is the substance of things hoped for, the evidence of things not seen." Hebrews 11:1

*****

Looking at the Dreaded List

Today I've finished three months of the year, a quarter of the way through. It's a good time to check on those twelve New Year's resolutions I made.

What! You've completed yours? Or did you just give up?

Without getting personal, here's my score so far:

1. Not going well, but still trying.
2. Not working out. Hoping for better days.
3. Success.
4. Have not started.
5. Working hard at it. Very difficult.
6. Success.
7. Doing okay, could be better.
8. Have not started.
9. Success. Must keep at it.
10. Pitiful.
11. Have not started.
12. Success.

You see, I've only succeeded in four of my twelve goals. I haven't given up on any of those changes yet, though half are on life support.

That's great! I'm better than I was on January 1, and that's really what I yearned for. I'm making progress, whether I actually accomplish all twelve goals this year or not.

And I've got a secret weapon:

"My God will supply all your needs, according to His riches in glory." Philippians 4:19.

*****

Empty Shelves

I guess I wasn't shocked. Maybe I was just surprised. I didn't expect to see Valentine candy for sale on December 27.

Most stores have a special section, near the door, reserved for seasonal and holiday merchandise. They know what's on your mind, and they want to be the first to offer you just what you need for that upcoming big day.

When Halloween is over, Thanksgiving will soon arrive, so stores replace the candy corn and scary masks with pilgrim and turkey items. When Thanksgiving is past (or almost), Christmas items replace the items that you needed for that fourth Thursday in November.

But Valentines goods right after Christmas? It seems ridiculous. Couldn't the stores just leave an empty shelf for a week or two? We have lost the idea of 'space in between,' or margins.

Maybe I'm 'the pot calling the kettle black.' Every Monday, I make a list of everything I'd like to get done in the upcoming week. Then I jump in and fill every minute, hoping to get everything on the list completed before the next Monday comes around. I never get it all done. There is no breathing room.

Psalm 46:10 reads, "Be still, and know that I am God." Maybe I thought it said, "Fly along, and know that I am God."

*****

Chapter Two: Growing Closer to God, Part One

We're not fully-mature Christians on the first day we're saved. God's Holy Spirit works to make changes over time. We need to do our best to cooperate!

Still Listening?

Beyond the noise of the encompassing crowd,
There comes a voice, near silent, not loud.
It calls to us like a trusted friend,
Offering love, our lives to mend.

We heard Him once, but He continues calling;
Years ago, Christ saved us from falling.
We closed our ears, for we'd done what we
    needed,
Having no time for a call that's repeated.

He offers us more, a lifetime together,
He wants to draw closer, not once but forever.
His grace is much more than a moment's
    transaction,
To only just taste is a puzzling reaction.

Relationship is what our God wants with us,
Each day should be building our faith and our
    trust.
Would a child stay a child, and refuse to grow?
When God would lead, would we refuse to go?

Seek the Lord, while He may be found.
Learn, and grow, make your foundation sound.
The closer you get to the God of the ages,
The fuller and happier are all of life's pages.
*****

When Is the Next Rainy Day?

One of those truths that I hold dear is, "If there is a horizontal surface in your house that has nothing on it, it won't stay that way for long." Corollaries include, "If there is still room in the attic, you don't have to get rid of it," and "As long as you have room, save it for a rainy day."

I suppose yard sales and flea markets depend on the attitude revealed in these old sayings. How many times have you seen something at a yard sale that you didn't know you needed it, until you saw it?

Now, stay with me here for a minute. In Matthew 12, Jesus talks about what happens when you get rid of "an unclean spirit." (Think addiction or bad habit, maybe.) When you clean that part of your life up, it is absolutely great! If you don't claim that space for something good, though, that unclean spirit will move back in, with some of its friends.

Empty spaces cause clutter. Cleaning expert Don Aslett says the biggest challenge to keeping a house clean is clutter. The answer is to convince yourself that you like that space empty, because you like your house clean and orderly, and extra stuff makes your house a lot harder to clean.

See the connection? When God cleans up a part of your life, learn to rejoice in it that way. Don't fill up the space with new stuff. God can keep the place cleaned up, if you don't work against Him.

*****

What's On Your Plate?

We have all heard that we are greater than we once were. That is, the people of our country are larger than they have ever been before. We are taking in more food than we use, and we are eating the wrong kinds of foods. Any extra intake we don't use is stored on our bodies as FAT.

In the same way, we are taking in the wrong kind of mental and spiritual food. How are we getting any nutrition from what we see on TV and in the movies, when we constantly make wrong 'food' choices? The murder and crime and secular vocal contests don't do much to energize our purpose in life, to serve God and bring people into His kingdom. The non-useful stuff is just FAT, getting in the way of the really good stuff.

What are you reading? I don't have to name authors and books for you to recognize that most best-sellers don't enhance your spiritual life. Get some real food! Let me suggest a few authors: Frank Peretti (especially his earliest books), Ted Dekker, Randy Singer, Brock and Bodie Thoene, Richard L. Mabry M.D., James L. Rubart, Lorena McCourtney, Terri Blackstock (not her early work). These fiction writers craft a great story, plus feed your soul.

Don't let me get started on music! Let it be enough to say, most people only make Christian music a minor part of their song library.

People leave churches every year because they are not being spiritually nourished. It puts a tremendous load on the pastor, Sunday School teacher, etc. to nourish folks enough in one day to counteract all the poor choices made on the other six!

*****

Expect Neglect

I can't plant a garden. I tried several times in the past, successfully, but I can't do it anymore.

And yet there is nothing like a fresh, homegrown tomato. Nothing!

Being a pastor doesn't go very well with gardening. There are times when I can set my own hours, and other times when I need to just drop what I'm doing and tend to a crisis. There are weeks when I've got an incredible work load, and other times when life flows at a calm, slower pace.

Gardens need regular attention. Mine gets neglect.

So, I settle for a few tomato plants. My limit is four plants. There is nothing like a fresh tomato. Tomatoes can stand a little neglect, especially if you put them in a container with a water reservoir.

There's a lesson there. If you don't set your expectations very high, in your relationship with God, you still may produce some great fruit. God has mercy! You may want to glance at your neighbor's 'garden,' though, and see how much more fruitful your life could be if you were to seek God with your whole heart.

*****

It's a Hard Job

It's hard being a Christian! Much of what Christ expects of us goes against our natural tendencies.

Even some of the joys of Christianity are hard. For instance, sharing God's love is hard. It's not hard to love family and friends, but it's kind of tough to go up to a visitor in church, introduce ourselves and treat them as if they were part of our family. "Love your neighbor as yourself."

If I were the visitor, it would make me feel good to have somebody come sit with me, help me know what's going on in the service and even introduce me to some of their friends. But I know that's hard. There's a lot of comfort in sitting in the same pew every week, quietly sensing God's presence. But sharing God's love is a great joy and privilege.

It's hard being a Christian. Christ expects us to not just 'go with the flow,' but to choose life. If we really take our Christian walk seriously, then there's nothing much to watch on TV, nothing much to see at the movies, nothing much for us on the New York Times bestseller list, and not many stations on the radio. Christ gives us abundant life, but we don't find it by 'going with the flow.'

It's hard being a Christian. It seems we always have to work at doing the Christian thing, going the Christian way, living the Christian life. Is it worth it? You bet! I know you've learned that, too! So don't be weary in well-doing. The best things in life are free, but they're not easy.

*****

Control Freak

Could it be that we've got a control problem?

For heaven's sake, when we became Christians, we asked Jesus to be our Lord. We asked Him to take control, to take the steering wheel, to be the driver in our life's journey. Ever since that day, we've been doing our best to not completely let go. How can we say we want Jesus to be Lord, and yet try to be in charge of what He gets to be in charge of?

It seems to me that giving the Lord control of our lives is a continuous thing. When we're first saved, we think we've totally given up being in control of our own lives, but every day we find another area we have not yet surrendered to Christ.

That's what the Bible means when it says to "work out your own salvation." Every day we must do the work of bringing His light to a new corner of our lives that has managed to stay in darkness.

We're more saved every day, and that's a good thing.

*****

Doing Life

Life is full of brush fires. There are always little emergencies to attend to. Only rarely does everything go right! Besides the emergencies, life is full of little duties. A lot of our time is spent on paying bills, being at the right place at the right time, making sure our children are at the right place at the right time. It's no wonder that many of us feel like we're not in charge of our lives. When will we get to do what WE want to do?

Force yourself to take at least an hour one day to decide what your mission in life is. If you don't know where you're going, how will you know when you get there? Rick Warren, author of The Purpose-Driven

<u>Life</u>, states the obvious: Your life is about pleasing God!

So how will you do that? Think it through, then write it down. It probably will sound something like this: "My mission is to live life abundantly as God's child, by serving God effectively as a (teacher, carpenter, preacher, husband, whatever)." Or maybe it will be more like, "My aim is to know God and follow God, in my home and at work and in my church." Then decide what steps you'll have to take to accomplish your life's mission, and decide what *Step One* is.

Now you're getting somewhere.

*****

Shortcuts

Life is full of shortcuts. Why do more work than you have to?

The shorter you can make a job, the more time left for other jobs. The easier you make your work, the less stress. The more you accomplish, the more other people are freed up to do more.

All this is true, yet it doesn't tell the whole story. Time is not an enemy that must always be subdued. Time has its friendly side! Some of the best things in life just take time.

Friendship with God takes time! There really are no shortcuts. Each minute you spend with God in prayer, you grow spiritually. Each hour in worship builds a foundation; your circumstances change, so what you experience in worship today might not hit you like it would have yesterday. And so forth...you get the idea.

Time spent witnessing, helping the needy, reading your Bible, praying, and in worship is priceless. You're investing in the abundant life Jesus promised. Don't take shortcuts!

*****

Wanting to Run

Okay. You've had that incredible call from God. You know exactly what God wants you to do in His service. What next?

Perhaps it's obvious that now is the time. For some of us, though, we can tell that God is wanting us to wait for the proper time.

What we really want to do is run, run to the battle, but God said to wait.

Remember how most footraces started when you were a kid? "Ready, set, go!" It was the only fair way to begin. If you just yelled, "Go!" you had an unfair advantage, and the race results didn't really count.

If God calls you, and says, "but wait," like he did when I was called into the ministry, the only sensible thing to do is get ready, then set, before you go. It may mean you need to study, or pray, or tie up loose ends. Once you're past the "ready' state, then just be set. Being set means staying on your mark, ready to take off at the perfect time. Now, that part is tough!

When you're ready, and set, waiting to go, that may be when you grow into one of Christ's greatest assets.

*****

The Tuxedo

In the back of my closet, I keep a black tuxedo. I've only worn it once. Yes, it's like new.

I had to buy it for the time I sang with the local college chorus (they invited singers from the community), in a performance of Handel's "Messiah."

You may assume that I keep it around for the memories. It certainly was a grand performance, though I was in over my head, 'the least of these.' No, I keep it for two reasons: First, I just may need a black tuxedo one day, and, second, it represents a standard size for me.

If I ever need a tuxedo, I want to be able to fit into it! The last time I tried it on, believe it or not, it was just about too big for me! I had just completed a diet. Thankfully, the pants have elastic in the waist.

On the other hand, we all have times when our weight inches up. The tuxedo represents my upper limit.

You may have guessed what religious ending I'm heading for with this. It's simply this: Jesus said,

"I am the way, the truth, and the life. No one comes to the father, but by me."

Jesus is my standard, and I won't let myself get too far away.

*****

Chapter Three: Faith

Can God do what the Bible says He did in the past? Can God do the miracles for us that friends claim He did for them? Faith is holding on to God's ability, believing that it is not different now than at any previous time.

The Sun Stood Still

I'm fascinated with the account in the Bible of the time that God extended a day, at Joshua's request. It's found in the book of Joshua, chapter ten.

The army of Israel had the upper hand in a battle, but daylight was going to run out before they could claim the victory. Joshua prayed that God would make the sun just stop, stay in place, and not let night come until the task was accomplished.

And God granted his request! The day was extended by another twenty-four hours.

Now, for those of us with a scientific bent, we immediately start thinking of all that would have to be fixed or tended to if the sun were stuck in the same place for an extra day. Our world is in an intricate (not precarious) balance. Much depends on the earth turning a complete revolution each day.

I have to be continually reminded that God is not limited. God still brings people back to life, makes diseases disappear, manages 'chance' meetings of people, keeps people from harm by changing their normal routines, and so much more. Eventually, maybe we will all stop selling God short.

"For nothing will be impossible with God." Luke 1:37

*****

Bright-Eyed

I'm an incurable optimist. I always see sunshine ahead.

I'm an unstoppable dreamer, rain ending with sunshine instead.

Losing must give way to winning, valleys make room for the mount.

I've got to live on the bright side, no caution lights or red.

How can folks keep looking downward, ignoring the good for the bad?

What is the fun in pessimism, not seeing the happy, but sad?

Why waste your time thinking failure, fishing around for mistakes,

Thinking of what has departed, counting the things that you had?

Sometimes it just takes a little, to go from "okay" up to "great."

You may need just minor assistance to climb to what's really top-rate.

Jesus has said He'll be with me, every step of the way.

So I go through my life just believing the best is my probable fate!

*****

Upside-Down World

I love roller coasters. It's not only the ones that go up tall hills and then swoosh you down to deep valleys that I like. I especially love the ones that take you backwards, upside down, and through high-speed turns and corkscrews.

Some people don't like roller coasters, for exactly the same reason I love them. There is a thrill involved, a perceived danger, a "what if there's a breakdown" recognition. It's living on the edge.

The chance of anything going wrong is incredibly small. Even so, for those who want to be in control of all the chances, roller coasters are a no-no.

Christians live on the edge. We know that there is always a chance of being ridiculed, persecuted, or even killed for your faith. You can minimize the chances by living a very quiet Christian life, never talking about Jesus, never helping the needy, not getting very involved in church or religious organizations.

God wants to turn your world upside-down, inside-out, and every which way. For some, that's too scary.

"Those who find their life will lose it, and those who lose their life for My sake will find it." Matthew 10:39

*****

Incomprehensible Faith

"Now faith is the substance of things hoped for, the evidence of things not seen." (Hebrews 11:1)

I suspect that faith is one of those things that our twenty-first-century minds just can't comprehend. We can understand the atom, flight, gravity and how our circulatory system works, but faith is one of those things we've got to use without having entirely mastered it.

Faith is the most powerful force in existence, because it brings to bear the power of God on our world. Faith is like a wall outlet, where we plug into the Power Source.

I Kings 18:41-45 tells of a time when Elijah prayed for rain. He had faith enough to tell the king, at the outset, "Get ready for an abundance of rain." Elijah began praying, and told his servant to look in the direction of the sea. After a little while, Elijah's servant said, "I see a little cloud, no bigger than a man's hand." Immediately, Elijah sent word to the king that, if he was going to travel, he'd better get in his chariot and go, before the roads got too muddy to allow passage.

I Kings 18:45 continues, "And it came to pass in the meanwhile, that the heaven was black with clouds and wind, and there was a great rain."

Imagine the faith it takes to know the smallest cloud is bringing rain for *you*. Think of the faith it takes to see a great result in our smallest beginning. A great faith can see a powerful man or woman of God in the first-time visitor to church or the smallest child. The most solid foundation for a great church is not stone or brick, but *faith*.

Expect great things when you plug into the Power Source.

*****

The Simple Cook

I've been cooking for most of my life.

Maybe it started when I was four or five, when the whole family would help Mom make her famous fruit salad for holiday gatherings. It took all of us! I can remember having the job of getting the seeds out of the grapes. (You thought the world always had seedless grapes?)

Grandma Luella had a diner, where I began cooking when I was in high school. She was a great cook and a great teacher!

I worked as a cook in a Denny's Restaurant in Media, Pennsylvania for a short time after graduating from college. It was great! It had a narrow, "alley" kitchen, built for speed.

My wife still lets me do some cooking. One thing baffles me, though: Spices. I tell you, if I have to get beyond salt, pepper, and granulated garlic, I'm lost. Any time I've used other spices, it is strictly by the command of some recipe. Adding additional spices on my own is a real journey into the unknown.

It is said that variety is the spice of life. In cooking, spices are the variety of life. They can really make a dish extra special.

Faith, in like manner, is a step into the unknown. It's scary. It takes a lot of leaning on God, and that's the part that God especially likes.

Hebrews 11:6 says, "But without faith it is impossible to please God."

Even God likes spice.

*****

Giant Killer

Maybe God just doesn't make men like David anymore.

In the story of David and Goliath, I just can't imagine me doing the same thing in that situation. Goliath challenged any Israelite soldier to fight him, one-on-one, winner take all. Goliath was almost twice David's height, with some fine armor. Good soldiers, known for courage and common sense, declined to take on the giant. Yet David never doubted he could win the contest, because he was standing "in the name of the Lord."

Maybe David hadn't really anticipated his bravery, either. He just happened on a situation where *somebody* needed to stand against evil in God's strength, and, well, it might as well be him.

When we come up against evil in our world, it may be a surprise or we may have advance notice. *Somebody* needs to stand against it! In our own strength, we'll be like those other soldiers, trembling and fearful. In God's strength, we'll defeat it.

Is there anyone that has enough faith in God to take on the evil of this world?

God *does* still make people like David. It might be you.

*****

Chapter Four: Love Your Neighbor

Jesus never passed by someone in need without helping them. We try to follow His example. It might be easier if we admitted to ourselves that serving others makes our own lives better.

Love Your Neighbor

It was a hot day, but Dave knew it had to be done. He had promised his son that he would put up a basketball goal, and today was the day Dave had reserved for doing it. He'd best get at it.

Dave figured out exactly where he needed to dig the hole for the post. He started digging with a pick and soon found out how little effort it would take today to work up a sweat. He waved at an old retired fellow going by in a pickup.

As he continued digging, now with a shovel, he paused a couple more times to wave at neighbors, who waved to him as they drove slowly by. This was really going to be work. Dave's t-shirt showed dark patches where perspiration had soaked through from the skin side.

About halfway deep enough now, he continued the hole with a post-hole digger. It was a little annoying to notice that a few people had gathered across the street, maybe to chat, but more likely to watch a young father do a bit of manual labor. Was this the biggest show in town?

Finally, Dave had dug the hole deep enough. He took the pick, shovel and digger back to the garage. With a great amount of effort, he dragged the sixteen-foot post back to the hole and contemplated what it would take to get it upright in the hole.

Across the street, half a dozen bystanders glanced in his direction. Dave looked at them. He shouted, "HEY! How about somebody giving me a hand?"

The watchers exchanged puzzled looks. And in answer to his request, they began to enthusiatically applaud.

Sometimes helping our neighbor goes beyond just encouraging.

*****

Just Out of Reach

It was a wonderful day in early March. The temperature had climbed to the eighties, and for once, the wind was not blowing.

I keep all my short-sleeved shirts hanging on a very high bar in the closet. It takes a tall step stool to reach them. When the weather gets warm, I swap them with the long-sleeved shirts, on the lower bar.

Was this the day to swap? I looked at the weather forecast for the next two weeks. No, it would not stay warm.

Sure would be a good day to wear a summer shirt. All it would take would be to walk the length of the house to the utility room, grab the step stool, bring it back to the closet, step up on it to reach a short-sleeved shirt, get it down, take the step stool back. It might take three minutes.

But those summer shirts were out of reach. Why go to the trouble?

I can think of a lot of thoughtful things we could be doing for other people, that would not take much time at all, but they never get done. I guess we're waiting for the right time, and it's always just out of reach.

*****

Not Me This Time

It's over.

All you really want to do is think about how awful life is now, how it will never be like it used to be, and how there is now an unfillable hole in your heart. All that kind of thinking centers on yourself. You've got to get out of that spiral toward depression.

It's not easy, but the best thing you can do to get over a major loss is to help somebody else. It has been proven to work wonders.

News flash: You don't have to be sad to be helped by thinking of others! It just makes sense that, if getting your mind off yourself helps when you're hurting, it ought to make you feel better even when you are not hurting.

It works. The happiest people are not the ones who have everything, but those who are constantly giving part of what they have to others. It takes energy to hold tight to things.

Luke 6:38 says, "Give, and it will be given to you. A good measure, pressed down, shaken together, running over, will be put into your lap, for the measure you give will be the measure you get back." I don't know if you've heard this before, but let me tell you now: The Bible has a lot of commands and guidelines, and they are all there to make your life better, not worse.

So give yourself away. You've got a lot to gain.

*****

A Measure of Love

Wisdom is looked for in the older generations. Why? Because wisdom comes from making mistakes and learning from them.

It would be wonderful if wisdom could be taught, and younger students would just take our word for what happens when a person makes certain mistakes. Not much wisdom is gained so simply.

By the time you get halfway through life, you learn that love must be parceled out carefully. Loving freely, with your whole heart, often brings great pain.

I've run across many Christians lately that have just not learned this lesson. They love without caution. It seems to work for them! Perhaps they have a limit, but if they do, it's far beyond what I would have expected.

I want to learn to love like that, don't you? It seems to do everyone around them a lot of good. In my heart, I know that God takes care of them, and gives them love that doesn't always get returned by their fellow humans. God takes care of the imbalance. It just takes a leap of faith.

John 13:35, "By this everyone will know that you are my disciples, if you have love for one another."

*****

No Thanks

Isn't it strange that the words "Thank you" have become less popular? The words just aren't heard as much anymore. Of course "Thank you" is not needed any less than in the past.

Oh, I know we hear those catchy little phrases at the big discount stores more than ever. "Thank you for shopping our _____," the girl says with a blank expression. As you leave, you see the little sign on the register: Don't forget to say "Thank you for shopping our _____." That's duty, not thanks.

It's just so hard for a society that prides itself in being self-sufficient to say thanks. We can hardly say "thank you" because that is admission that we didn't handle everything ourselves. (In the same way, we have a hard time acknowledging God's help.)

Saying thank you is *not* an admission of our own weaknesses. It's a chance to build our sister or brother up. It's part of that "love your neighbor as yourself" stuff, part of the Goldnen Rule. In Hebrews 10:24, we read,

"And let us consider how to provoke one another to love and good deeds."

*****

Too Much Truth

The truth hurts. Sometimes I just don't want to hear it.

In fact, I rebel against hearing the truth from those who seem to love to hurt me with it, wielding the truth like a Viking battle axe. I'll bet you can agree with that! How many scars do you have from times people bluntly spoke truth to you "as a friend," with no trace of friendliness? I close my ears to truth that enjoys 'slicing and dicing' me or someone else.

I know, though, that the truth is good for us. Godly advice can protect us from future harm. A true friend can reveal truth to us that we are somehow blind to. That friend, however, had better bring it with a bucket of love.

The more jarring the truth is expected to be to the hearer, the bigger the bucket of love we must bring with it.

*****

Handling the Weeds

So, explain the part in the Bible that says not to pull the weeds out of your garden.

In Matthew 13:24-30, there is a parable about a grain field that has sprouted weeds. The hired hands go to the farmer and say, "Didn't you plant good seed? There are weeds coming up in your grain field. Do you want us to pull the weeds?"

The farmer says, "No, let them grow awhile. Pull the weeds at harvest time, before we cut the grain, when it's easy to tell the difference. If you pull them now, you'll damage the roots of the grain."

Now, when I was a kid, my dad would never let us get away with not weeding the garden. Don't expect to do any fun stuff if you haven't weeded your part of the garden.

The weeds would steal nutrients from the vegetable plants!

There are many activities you pursue regularly that steal 'nutrients' from your spiritual growth. However, don't assume that everything that's not church-related or Bible-centered is a weed! Wait a little while. It could be that God wants to use that pursuit as common ground for you to reach someone for His kingdom. A conversation about college football, cooking, astronomy or whatever can sometimes lead to conversation about God.

If God says yank out a weed, don't hesitate! Just remember: Humans are notoriously bad at knowing a weed from something more valuable.

*****

Leave Me Alone

I'm impressed with how easy it is to be alone.

If a person really wanted to, he could live a life that really limited relationships. It's not that hard anymore. For instance, just a few years ago, everyone was known by the local postmaster. You at least had to go buy some stamps every now and then!

Now you can do that online. Prepaid boxes for mailing can also be bought in the same way, so it is not necessary to even have the postmaster weigh a package.

All your banking can be done without going to the institution in person. Clothing, books, prescription drugs can all be acquired without leaving the home. If you actually shop in person, it can be so rare that no cashier or associate recognizes you!

Many smaller stores have been unable to compete with the retail giants. So much of our shopping is now done in stores where we rarely see the same employees more than once in a year.

I think it is now easier to live a solitary life than one enriched by relationships. How sad.

God calls us to a life full of relationships. "Love your neighbor as yourself." "Go to all the world and make disciples." We need each other!

Seems like God's adversary has discovered the old military strategy, 'divide and conquer.'

*****

Big Visits

It's amazing how powerful the act of visiting another person is becoming. Have you noticed?

We don't visit other people like we used to, and there are many good reasons for it. For one, most everybody has air conditioning, so we keep our windows and doors closed, and people don't sit out on the porch at the end of the day. People work longer and unusual hours, so sometimes we don't know when a good time to visit would be. We've lost our knack for small talk or light conversation; people keep to themselves even when they are with other people, with earphones on or with one ear to the telephone. Lots of people have gates or unlisted telephone numbers (or their line is always busy).

So even an occasional visit to a person becomes a big event. They stop everything and spend more time than they thought they had when you come by. They tell their friends about it the next day. They remember everything you talked about. You become much more important in their life.

I encourage you to find time to visit somebody you don't know very well. Make time by missing one of the Atlanta Braves telecasts, or go on one less shopping errand, or put off a little of the laundry until tomorrow. Your visit can be an example of God's love and care.

*****

This Job Stinks. I Don't Mind.

Surely it's an unpleasant job.

I went to the dentist this week, to get a lost filling replaced. The tooth didn't hurt, but the filling had fallen out a few weeks ago and needed replacing.

First, the doctor gave me a shot to numb the area and he stepped out to give some time for the shot to take effect.

Anyway, as I sat in the chair, I thought, "Surely being a dentist is an unpleasant job. They spend hours a day, looking inside mouths, at decay, at chipped and broken teeth and at deteriorating fillings. I suppose some patients even have bad breath! What a job."

Yet dentists are cheerful. They must find satisfaction in helping patients get their smile and their 'eating machine' back in order.

There is a parallel with our jobs as ambassadors for Christ. We are to be "about our Father's business," helping the lost and

50

hurting around us get their lives back in order, and helping people restore a broken-down relationship with God.

It may look to be an unpleasant job. As we act as God's instrument to restore and clean up lives, we may find ourselves helping to handle a lot of bad-smelling trash. Yet we have great joy as Christians when we see lives and relationships restored.

It's not really such a bad job. It has great rewards. It just may look unpleasant to those not involved.

Being an ambassador for Christ *is* your job.

*****

Look Who's With Us!

I needed to make a hospital visit early yesterday morning, to the suburbs of Atlanta. Right after an early breakfast, I headed up the interstate.

I really love driving on the interstate. I understand that some folks are just the opposite, avoiding it at any cost, always choosing the road less traveled. I always choose the road greatly traveled.

Between 7 and 9 am, most of the traffic heading toward Atlanta consists of people heading to work in that great city. They range from the patient, cautious type to the weaver, who is always looking for a chance to move up a few car lengths. All of us are at the speed limit or slightly above.

I noticed a driver in the middle of the three lanes, car obviously on cruise control, that had her visor down. That was odd for a cloudy day. When I saw the little visor lights, I realized she was putting on makeup, traveling down the interstate at 75 miles per hour. Perhaps that wasn't the safest way to drive.

That's not my point, though. Most of us have done something similar, like talking on the phone or reading emails or eating a big sandwich while driving. The point is that driving on the interstate, especially near a big city, takes a lot of faith, not just in God, but in each other. We all have to take care of each other, because not all of us are at our best at any given moment.

That's my idea of the church. None of us are perfect, but we travel together, taking care of each other as we head for our destination.

*****

Time for Friends

It's crazy, I guess, but at times I've told folks that it looks like I don't have time for friends.

Friends take time, don't they? You've got to take time to keep up with each other's lives. You've got to care when they're sick, you've got to rejoice together, you've got to share a meal every now and then. It all takes time.

On the other hand, there is nothing like a friend when you are down. There's nothing like a friend when you've been lonely. There's nothing like a friend when this old world picks you off your feet, throws you down, and stomps all over you.

A friend is someone you can run to with good news, so it doesn't nearly burst inside of you. It takes a friend to listen when you finally understand what life is all about, and you just need to say it out loud to someone, so you know you really have understood it yourself.

If you've ever had a good friend, you know that you will always make time for them, somehow, someway.

Thank God for friends!

*****

Not Nice Jesus

Jesus was not a nice man.

What do we mean when we characterize someone as nice? I guess I picture someone who smiles a lot, who never says anything inappropriate, who does those little things that are expected and sweet. I also think of a nice person as one who lives a life that doesn't upset anybody. My buddy Webster says nice means "agreeable, pleasant, delightful; courteous and considerate; conforming to approved social standards."

Jesus was not a nice man. He was very loving, very honest, very sincere. He cared deeply for each and every person. He never excluded anyone, no matter what their social status was. But nice? No.

I struggled to be nice when I was a teenager. I tried to be "agreeable, pleasant, delightful; courteous and considerate." I wanted to conform, to fit in. Instead, I should have tried harder to be caring, honest, sincere, and loving.

A nice church, I suppose, is agreeable, pleasant and conforms to approved social standards. A church that seeks to share Christ won't necessarily be nice. It will be Christ-like; caring for those in need, standing up for the truth and reaching out with love to one and all.

Have a nice day. No, I guess what I mean to say is, may God bless you this day as the love of Christ is shed abroad in your heart.

*****

Chapter Five: Growing Closer to God, Part Two

We'll never be perfect, but the more we know Jesus, the more we'll know life.

Getting Things Done

Days just fly by, don't they? We've nearly finished another year. I've heard it said that the older you get, the faster the years go by. Is that true?

As we swiftly travel through this life of ours, every once in a while we have occasion to look back and summarize: What have I done worthwhile so far? It can be depressing. Hardly anyone has accomplished as much as they had hoped. Yet it is healthy and necessary to see where we've been

The more we've accomplished in our lives, the better we feel about ourselves. The secret to accomplishing much is simple: Plan, set goals and decide the steps you'll take to meet your goals. Nearly every time management seminar you can take boils down to the same scheme, though they may employ different gimmicks.

Have you grown in your spiritual life? Maybe you had the crazy idea that growth is automatic! You need to plan a course of action, set goals, decide steps you need to take. Examples: Learn to pray, learn what's in the Bible, learn to share your faith. How can you accomplish these goals? You can decide on a plan of action, if you'll give it a try, then plan what steps will get you to the goal. If you have trouble, ask your pastor or a more experienced Christian for help.

Don't let the years slip by without growing in Christ. The Christian life can be a feast. Why spend your whole life on the appetizers?

*****

Feast

Restaurants are teaching us to be do-it-yourself taxidermists. The portions they give us are much more than we really need, and we "stuff" ourselves.

Often we regret overindulging ourselves later, because we gain weight; it's much harder to lose weight than it is to put it on. In fact, the Bible calls gluttony (willful overeating) a sin, and we *should* have regrets about it!

Gluttony is acceptable in one area of our lives, though, and is actually encouraged. Ephesians 5:18 says to "be filled with the Spirit." Go ahead, get all of God you can. Fill up beyond the point at which most people stop.

Have you ever watched someone suffer at a buffet or Thanksgiving meal or a family feast, because they just couldn't allow themselves to eat very much? Sometimes it's because they're on a diet, or perhaps their doctor has forbidden certain foods. They really suffer, while the rest of the guests are having a great time.

God lays out a great spiritual feast for us, from the Bible to prayer to worship --- and many other great 'casseroles' and 'desserts.' This is no time to diet! Don't hold back! Blessed is the person who can shout exuberantly, "I'M FULL!"

*****

There Was Once a Man...

I've become my own sermon illustration. "I knew this guy one time,..."

Today I weigh eight more pounds than I did seven weeks ago. It's not fair. I get exercise and I eat healthy foods. I do almost everything you should do to stay at the same weight. Almost everything.

Nobody should have to give up everything, just to keep the same weight and the same clothing sizes.

But it doesn't work that way. The thing we don't want to give up is our main problem.

Is ice cream really that bad? I love ice cream, all flavors. And just a little ice cream is cruel, like a kiss on the cheek when you want a big smackeroo.

So I'm counting calories again, and getting extra exercise. I have loved ice cream, these seven weeks, more than a comfortable fit for my clothes.

Most Christians, I suppose, have a similar situation. They live for God, obeying the Bible, avoiding sin...except for that one. You know what I'm talking about, though it's a different sin for each person. There is one area you just won't give God control over. "But God, I'm perfect in anything else." It's that one little thing that you hang on to, something that you really like to do, something that defines who you are.

But if you keep control over part of your life, God is not really getting a chance to remake you. Your heart is not really completely sold on being made in His image.

And that's the bottom line. God wants all of you. God wants your heart.

*****

The Old Nose Problem

My pet and exercise buddy, Alfie, got bit on the nose by a snake last Friday. He spent four days at the animal hospital, recovering from that misadventure.

Alfie is twelve years old, otherwise known as "old enough to know better." He has a streak of curiosity, which is wonderful on our daily walks, since he finds some incredible and crazy places to lead me. In four years living in Albany, Georgia, he never took me on exactly the same route twice. There were new streets or alleys, unauthorized shortcuts across yards, dashes under low tree limbs at high speed, sudden switchbacks to chase a cat or squirrel, and mad dashes home at the sound of thunder.

One antic that was usually (not always) fun, was his putting on all four of his brakes at once, when he smelled something especially intriguing. I would, of course, stop as quick as I could, but sometimes I would reach the end of the leash before my

60

momentum got under control, and find myself flat on the ground. Smells always got his attention. Even a dried-up chicken bone that someone had discarded under a bush would not escape the powers of his nose.

Occasionally his nose gets him into trouble. Once a sprinkler came on, just as he put his nose up to it. Another time, he grabbed a kitten in his mouth from under a bush. I pounded him on the side quite forcefully, and he let it go without damage, but the mother cat was furious. Alfie just barely escaped that encounter unscathed.

So this time his nose got him in trouble. My wife and I were gone for a few hours, and when we got home, we were astounded by how swollen Alfie's head was. We called the vet, and rushed him on in, just before closing time. His doctor concluded it was a snake bite.

There's a lesson there for all of us, of course. We get our 'noses' into all kinds of places we shouldn't, and usually suffer no permanent damage. The Bible calls it "enjoying sin for a season." Sometimes, though, we get bit. We have no one to blame but ourselves.

*****

Eat More Steak

I grilled two beautiful steaks today, a gift from a friend.

I have two small grills, one charcoal and one propane. The charcoal grill takes a little preparation. On the other hand, I wasn't sure if the propane grill had enough fuel left to cook a steak. So I decided to cook one steak on each grill.

I poured charcoal into the charcoal grill, piled the pieces into a pyramid, doused it with lighter fluid, and ignited it. I usually wait at least a half hour for the charcoal to settle down to beautiful cooking coals.

Meanwhile, I started the propane grill and put a steak on it. It was well done in fifteen minutes. Due to my superior organizational skills (!!!), the rest of the meal was ready and on the table by the time the steak from the propane grill was ready. I divided the steak between my wife and I, and we sat down to a lovely meal. The second steak, on the charcoal grill, cooked while we ate.

Now, ordinarily we would have a steak each. However, when the second steak from the charcoal grill was finished, we were full! What's wrong with this picture?

Joy and I have not eaten many steaks lately. In fact, I think this may be the first we've had this year. And when you're just not used to eating steak, you just can't eat a lot of it.

There's a connection there with your walk with God, isn't there? When you're not used to serious work in growing closer to God, it doesn't take much to satisfy you. When daily devotions are seven minutes, when Bible study is just those few verses from Sunday's sermon, when "love thy neighbor" is just a few bucks in the Salvation Army kettle in December, you'll find you won't be looking to put much of God in your life. That's a huge loss. You might say that God is the 'steak' in life, and people settle for cold cereal.

*****

Mountain Top Experience?

It's been a great week in the mountains with some very good clergymen friends. We've had some wonderful meals together, spent time hiking to and from some magnificent waterfalls, and had time to share deep conversation.

I suppose the talk was the main part. This was not a vacation, but a time apart to share, encourage, rehabilitate, and de-stress.

God was in the middle of each conversation.

For me, there was an added feature. I didn't sleep well, and that was God's doing. God had a chance to get me alone at the very end of each day, like a father having a one-on-one talk with one of his boys. I needed badly to be corrected in certain areas of my relationship with my heavenly Father and, well, a good parent does not pass up golden opportunities to guide their offspring.

No, I hadn't done anything terribly wrong. God just needed to stop me from beating myself up about things I couldn't accomplish, that He never meant me to pursue. There were other avenues to walk that I hadn't even noticed.

So, you see, a "mountain top experience" may not always be joyous. It may be simply life-changing.

*****

Put the Car in Gear

I just finished one of those ten-week Bible study courses, including daily workbook assignments and a two-hour weekly group session. Whew! It took a lot of dedication for all of us. The fellowship was great, both the light chatter and the deep sharing. We'll start another study in a couple months.

What becomes of those Bible studies? Do they really change anything?

When my wife and I moved a few months ago, I had to sort through my office files. Why move anything that is no longer useful? One section of files was notes and notebooks from twenty-three years of continuing education seminars I attended for work. Considering that I attended an average of two seminars per year, there were a lot of files to sort through. I was amazed how little of that volume of files was still relevant!

With the perspective of a few years, things that seemed important at one moment can be recognized as much less than timeless after a little while. Life needs regular sorting through!

How do we assure that what we learn today will keep its relevance? You know the answer: Use it!

So, in this time between Bible studies, my responsibility is to put into practice what God has taught me in the last ten weeks. If it was important enough to invest my time in, it's too important to just toss in the junk pile later.

Blessed by Aggravation

I'm thankful for aggravation from God. What a blessing!

I don't always enjoy being taught by God. Did you enjoy every teacher you had in school?

Yet it was the most aggravating teachers I remember most. They were the ones who would not let me just be a good, or even great, student. They wanted the best out of me. It did not matter if I was doing "A" work; they wanted "A plus."

A seminary professor comes to mind at this point. I was really struggling in a New Testament class, but was really giving it extra effort. We had a ten-page paper due, midway through the semester. I wanted to make a big impression, so I looked up some Greek words and got definitions out of a concordance. I used this as a foundation for the paper, then launched into some very good and intricate arguments.

Well, I got a very low grade on that paper. I was shocked! The professor let me know that the definition of a key Greek word I used was faulty, very clearly off in a wrong direction. Though I had not had a course in Biblical Greek, I assumed I could find all the Greek I needed in a reference book. That key lesson sticks with me. The poor grade hurt at the time, but it was very helpful in the long run.

I am thankful for God's never-ending pushing and pulling and prodding. His Spirit in me is an incredible teacher. I really do want to get better every day, even when I stop for rest at times.

*****

Not Routine

The older I get, the more I cling to routine. It gives me comfort. I like having order in my life.

Still, life is about change. When I stop allowing myself to change, I'm convinced I'll start allowing myself to die. Know what I mean? I've got to keep my mind working, my body moving, my heart feeling emotion. I've got to keep my life full o f freshness.

I want my spiritual life to be fresh, too. I want to keep seeking to know God better. I want to hear from God in prayer. I want to find new ways to serve Him. I'm looking for fresth ways to tell others what He's done for me.

God gives me life, and I want to live it more abundantly each day.

*****

Starting Again

Vacation is wonderful, and essential. It sure ruins routine, as it is supposed to.

I had just gotten back into a lot of good habits. I've been lifting weights three times a week for twenty minutes. I've been faithful to writing something three times a week. I'm back on a diet, getting my eating habits in proper order.

And then comes vacation.

I can guarantee that my exercise routine will get all out of whack. Riding in the car from 8 am to 6 pm doesn't leave much time for physical activities. The snacks in the car and at the stops along the way will not be my regular fare, with less fruits and vegetables, more carbohydrates. And, believe it or not, my dad does not own a computer, and has a very poor signal for our phones and tablets (that's country living).

I'll do the best I can. I understand, though, that I will have to start again on many things when I get home again.

Life is full of restarts. Some folks can't handle that well, and waste a lot of time complaining about the disruption. The quicker we can get back to a routine that includes all our good habits, the happier we'll be.

Starting over is God's specialty, by the way. God always forgives your waywardness, and will give you a clean slate when you ask. Leave the past behind, and start a new and better routine today. And don't try to do it all on your own strength, when God is always here to lean on.

*****

Chapter Six: Forgiveness

A simple explanation for forgiveness is unshackling two people from opposite poles of an unpleasant event they've shared.

God Forgets?

Does God forget our trespasses? Well, not exactly. God is not absent-minded. Psalm 103:12 says that God removes our sins from us "as far as the east is from the west." Yet God knows us inside and out.

It's not the remembrance of what someone does against us that is the problem; it's the emotions connected to the remembrance. The emotions can cause a distance between friends.

Let me illustrate this. You throw a party, and a close friend says he'll be there. Well, he never shows up and you're hurt. If you say you forgive him, and don't invite him to any more parties, it's not God's kind of forgiveness. When God forgives our sins, he doesn't forget them, but He doesn't allow them to affect future relations with you.

You are just as loved as if you had never sinned.

Forgive me, Lord, and let me surprise You when I don't do that same sin again.

*****

Faulty Heroes

The Old Testament doesn't pull any punches. The heroes in our faith history were often prone to making mistakes. The Old Testament doesn't leave those mistakes out of the story.

For each of the Ten Commandments, we can easily find examples of what happens when the commandment is violated. For instance, "Do not commit adultery" was ignored by David in his 'fling' with Bathsheba, and the consequences troubled him for decades. "Honor your father and your mother" was obeyed by neither Eli's sons nor Samuel's sons, and the country fell into being led by a king instead of directly by God. Jacob's life was a mess because he did not obey "Do not covet."

Why put all these failures in the Bible? We need heroes, not scoundrels, right? I suspect the most important two reasons are, first, to see how foolish it is to choose not to obey God's guidance, and second, to show God can use even the most mistake-prone human to accomplish great things.

*****

Chapter Seven: Prayer

Prayer is simply talking to God. However, conversation can be very difficult when you are speaking to someone you are in reverent awe of.

Tell Me Nothing

A telephone conversation can be very important, even when you have nothing to say.

Sure, you've just talked to your dad or sister or friend last week. You've got nothing to say now. No big event has occurred in the last seven days. Still, you would just like to hear their voice.

Many of us keep contact with friends and relatives through social media. It has really changed my life! A lot of things cannot be said via Facebook or Twitter, and perhaps it paints a rosier picture of our lives than is really the case. But in many cases, it's enough.

Of course, not everyone is into social media. Some of my relatives don't even have a computer! And sometimes, you really want to hear a certain someone's voice.

But what if you have nothing to say?

I may not talk to Dad more than once a month, but I need to hear his voice. What seems ordinary to him is big news to me, like his participating in two bowling leagues (plus the monthly one). After all, Dad is eighty-six! Asking how his brothers and sisters are doing is important to me, even if nothing much has changed. When I have nothing new to tell him, he enjoys knowing that life is going on an even keel for me.

Love your neighbor as yourself, or as the Golden Rule says, Do unto others as you would have them do unto you. Tell them nothing, and enjoy hearing their nothing in return.

*****

Coffee of the Soul

Coffee and I have been close friends for years. Sometimes we have perhaps been too close. When I get beyond two quarts in one day, my muscles start to twitch!

Nothing compares to the aroma of black coffee, and there is no better hand warmer than a mug of hot coffee held between your hands.

74

I love the taste. That's why I don't use cream or sugar in my coffee; that would lessen the coffee taste.

Most of all, I think most of us love coffee for the way it makes our drowsiness disappear. After a little coffee, I am much more aware of the things around me. Pre-coffee, I can miss a lot.

I need spiritual coffee, too, something that will open my eyes to all God is doing around me. I need a little jolt, you know?

My spiritual coffee is found in my morning prayer time. Like anybody else, part of my prayer is laying my needs before God, asking for help and guidance, but that's not the spiritual coffee. It's when I get quiet, and let God speak to me, that I get my needed jolt. Sometimes God speaks words to my heart, sometimes I sense His direction in a decision that is coming up, and sometimes it's just feeling God's presence in the silence.

It's spiritual coffee, knowing God is there with me. I've got to have it every morning. So far, I haven't found a limit that will make my muscles twitch!

*****

Tell Me How to Pray

Ever have anybody ask you how to pray? I have. What do you tell them?

Prayer is conversation with God, plain and simple. You talk to God in your own way. (Do you think that if you prayed like Billy Graham or Charles Stanley, God wouldn't recognize that it was really you, the one He considers His priceless treasure?)

You don't have to use long words, or be pretentious. Just consider that God is a friend who is right here, right now, and is hanging on your every word. ("Ask and it will be given you, seek and you shall find, knock and the door will be opened unto you", Luke 11:9.) Remember, of course, that in any conversation, you ought to be careful to listen for what the other party has to say. God may surprise you!

I hate to burst your bubble, but praying out loud in church or for some other group isn't a fine art that few can learn. The more your public prayer can still be an intimate conversation with God (with the congregation listening in and agreeing), the more honest it is. God doesn't want a show; God wants to know your heart.

✣ ✣ ✣ ✣ ✣

Time to Pray

There is a time for prayer. People differ, of course, as to when it's time to pray. Some pray all the time. Some rarely pray.

Those that rarely pray feel that God has given us a brain and abilities and talents, so that we can handle most everyday situations. "Use what God has given you. Don't bother God about little things." That way of thinking reveals a basic misunderstanding of prayer. It's not a request line for help, but conversation between two friends.

Those that pray all the time don't do it out of a lack of ability, or fear of facing life head-on. Constant prayer is a sharing of life with the One who is always with you. Even when the conversation isn't put into words, there is a recognition of God's presence. You know what that's like, don't you? Some friends you can feel so comfortable with that you don't have to fill every silence with words.

Do those that pray constantly still call on God in times of crisis? You can be sure of it! Any close friend reveals all his struggles to his friend. God is a friend who is able to help us with anything that comes up, and is too close a friend to stand idly by. And, like the closest of friends, He won't let us settle for the easy way out.

Prayer is not a sign of weakness, but a sign of closeness.

*****

All You Need

Philippians 4:19 says, "God will supply all your needs, according to His riches in glory."

Sounds great! God's riches will never run out, so I guess Christians can spend, spend, spend, right? Well, not exactly.

Our needs will be supplied. That's really not very exact, for we usually have trouble telling needs from wants. Often our needs are determined by the lifestyle we've chosen. We choose to live at a particular level, which requires a certain income and particular possessions. The president of a major corporation claims needs that I would consider luxuries; some of my own needs look extravagant to a poor person.

God has a plan for your life, and if you get in on that plan, you will see that God will supply everything necessary, plus an incredible number of extra blessings.

*****

Chapter Eight: Maintaining, Part One

Okay, you've been a Christian for awhile now. You are 'comfortable in your own skin.' At this point, you are about to find out that if you're not growing closer to God, you are slipping farther away. There is no resting place.

Comfort Is a Moving Target

It's hard to live a comfortable life. Maybe it's the times we live in, I don't know.

If we agree on the basic idea that happiness, or comfort, doesn't really come from the things we own, then we will probably agree that a comfortable life comes from our relationships. That's why life just isn't comfortable.

Relationships will, if just left alone, gradually change. Whether it's our relationship with family, friends, relatives, or even with God, constant and vigorous maintenance is required to keep our relationships strong. Maybe that's something we try not to admit to ourselves. We'd prefer to find a comfortable point in life where we could do nothing, and still relationships would not change.

Take a good look at your relationship with God. Maybe it's time to get back in the game.

*****

Loving the Torture

Does it ever bother you that the outstanding symbol of our Christian faith is the cross?

We see past the torture. Death by crucifixion would be considered inhumane today. The public suffering involved was meant to serve as a deterrent to crime, especially the crime of inciting revolution against the Roman Empire.

But we see the joy on the other side. Jesus died to pay the penalty for our sins. If we take that death as payment for our own sins, God promises eternal life.

But there's more! The cross is a symbol of how we are to live. The vertical beam represents our relationship to God, and the horizontal beam represents our relationship with other people. Of course, the vertical component is longer, because it's more important.

Luke 10:25-28 reinforces this: "Just then a lawyer stood up to test Jesus. "Teacher," he said, "what must I do to inherit eternal life?" He said to him, "What is written in the law? What do you read there?" He answered, "You shall love the Lord your God with all your heart, and with all your soul, and with all your strength, and with all your mind; and your neighbor as yourself." And he said to him, "You have given the right answer; do this, and you will live.""

*****

Dampen My Day, Not My Spirits

I had all kinds of plans for today, but it's raining. It's raining a lot.

When will I do all that good stuff I had planned? You can't do yard work in the rain. Shopping in a big city can be treacherous in the rain. Even walking the dog is ill-advised.

I kind of pouted inside myself for a few hours, I admit it. I finally decided to fight back!

Reading, it is said, is a way to visit places without leaving your home. It works! I actually just caught up reading the local papers.

Music lifts your spirits above the clouds. I took it a step further with Christian pop music, lifting me heavenward.

I took time, while it was raining, to write to some friends. That got me out of my rainy little world and into theirs.

It surely is a waste of time, wishing you were someplace else. It's easy to do that on a rainy day. How many hours, days, and lifetimes are wasted thinking about what's wrong with where you are, instead of making the most of what's right about present circumstances?

Live every day, even the rainy ones.

*****

What Is It?

In Exodus 16, we read about one of those days when the Hebrew people that Moses was leading out of captivity 'got up on the wrong side of the bed.' They were grumpy. Even though they had been delivered by God from slavery, they were complaining.

The people were hungry. They said to Moses, "Why have you led us out into the wilderness, to die of hunger? We wish we'd stayed in Egypt, where at least we could have died with a full belly."

Moses got a message from God, "I'll send bread from heaven for the people." So Moses passed on the message, that God would send them bread and tomorrow "they would see the glory of the Lord." That night God caused an abundance of quail to land at their camp and they ate meat.

In the morning, on the ground was a great amount of a kind of wafer, which we know was the 'manna' that God would begin to supply daily for their bread. But when the Hebrew people saw the new substance, they said, "What is it?" (That's what manna means.)

God had said He'd supply bread for them. Moses told them to expect to see "the glory of the Lord." And there it was. And they didn't know what it was!

In the Lord's Prayer, which we pray often, we ask God to supply our needs (our daily bread). Many church services include this every week. I'm convinced that God answers our prayers. Yet many times we see God's provision and wonder, "What is it?" Maybe God provides for us in a way we're not looking for and we stand looking 'like a dog at a new dish.'

Think for a minute, right now, how God has supplied your needs -- your 'daily bread.'

Look carefully. Let's not be those who say, "What is it?" but those who say, "Thank you, Lord!"

*****

Beach Life

I spent a few days with some clergy friends at the beach this week. I always consider these retreats as more necessary for my friends than for myself. Inevitably, though, I find out that I needed those days more than I realized.

What is it about the beach that provides healing for the soul? It's not the tanning power of the sun, since my kind of tan (a bright red color) is more trouble than therapy. Perhaps some of the healing is people watching; we quickly discover that there are more average people than magazine models sharing the sand with us. When the beach is pretty deserted, though, the healing power is still there.

I was walking the beach by myself a few days ago, just before sunset. The waves came rushing in from far, far away. The ocean seemed to have no end. The sky was a rich blue, no clouds in sight. The healing I felt was from my recognizing the presence of God.

Can a person get the same therapy from spending time in the mountains? Maybe. I think some find it in biking, or hiking, or even on long drives by themselves. Some, I think, have found similar healing in staying at home.

Need some healing?

"Be still, and know that I am God." Psalm 46:10

*****

Saving Books

Over the span of twenty-four years in the ministry of the United Methodist Church, I've moved six times. Many fine church members have toted boxes and other paraphernalia in and out of parsonages for us on our moving days.

What they remember most is carrying boxes of books. More than anything else, we have books. We don't throw away books, and we rarely give them away or sell them.

If you were to look through the books my wife and I have, you would learn lots about us, even just looking at the titles. For instance, Joy has math books, organic food books, homeschooling books, etc I've got a juggling book or two, Bible commentaries, books about baseball, etc. We have hundreds of Christian novels.

Why do we keep them? Are we going to read them all again? That would be impossible, with all we have. Books represent knowledge to us, good stories, good memories. They are a slice of who we are.

The best-selling book of all time, by far, is the Bible. It's all the above- knowledge, good stories, good memories. Yet it's so much more. The Bible is truth, God's Word, and a guide for life. I've only given away one Bible in my life, a study Bible that was so worn the cover was falling off. The man I gave it to understood its value, and bound up all its broken places, and really brought a smile to my face when he showed me the repairs.

"Thy word is a lamp unto my feet, and a light unto my path." Psalm 119:105

*****

Giving Thanks Today

Thank you, God.
    Hands, feet, eyes, ears, taste.
    Your many gifts I often waste.

Thank you, God.
    Family, neighbors, many a friend.
    I wish I did all that I did intend.

Thank you, God.
    Work, play, time alone.
    There's too many things that I
          condone.
Thank you, God.
    Worship, Bible, service, prayer.
    I ought to take you everywhere.

Thank you, God.
    You give us so much.
    And your mercy endures forever.
        *****

You've Changed

It's been a long time. Maybe it's been forty years, I don't know. I've lost track.

Your face is different, that's it. No, not your hair. It doesn't bother me that it's gray now instead of blonde.

No, it's not the wrinkles. We all get them, some from frowning, some from smiling, all from growing older. That's no big deal.

You smile more now. That's the difference. I don't think it's because you're richer because, frankly, nobody seems to end up with a lot of extra money, no matter how much they make. The more we make, the more we spend.

Really, nothing on the outside that you could do could possibly make you look as good as you do now. Your smile is from deep within, soul deep. You have found something that so many seem to miss, and so they will never radiate like you.

You've found the meaning of life. You've found Jesus. Jesus looks good on you.

"In Him was life, and the life was the light of all people." John 1:4

*****

Satisfaction

Satisfaction guaranteed? Sure, buddy. There doesn't seem to be such a thing anymore. Satisfaction is a commodity we don't seem to understand.

On the other hand, we understand quite well what it means to have 'more' or want more or do more. More is a driving force in our society.

I think we have disassociated the words *more* and *excess*. You and I know that excess is bad. It can kill you. Too much of anything can lead to physical or financial or emotional or spiritual ruin. Although we know that excess is to be avoided like the plague, somehow we've forgotten that excess is a result of our drive for more.

Yet we continue to strive for more. The only way to stop before we reach the point where more turns into excess is to recognize satisfaction. Intuitively, or maybe because of the Holy Spirit in us, we know that God gives us ways to know when we've reached satisfaction. "Come unto me, all you who are weary and heavy laden, and I will give you rest." Matthew 11:28 Man, wouldn't that be nice, to reach a point of rest? To have "the peace that passes understanding"? *Philippians 4:7*

If we're honest, we can probably tell when our wants exceed our needs. And then we need to decide what we'll do with the excess, when we accumulate more than we need. Do you have a plan? What will you do with sudden unexpected income? Time? Joy? Without a plan, you'll keep it, and excess kills.

Of course, our greatest gift is eternal life, more good news than we deserve. Have you a plan to share the Good News?

*****

Chapter Nine: The Church

The church is not a building, but a gathering of people. These people get together to worship God, to serve other people, for study, and for fellowship. It is not without faults. God is faithful to continue working to improve the church.

What's Cooking, God?

I love to make the empty-the-refrigerator kind of soup. Whether you call it soup or stew, it's amazing how tasty a combination can be made by putting together a meat and a wild variety of vegetables.

God does that. Look at our churches! We've got people of various educational backgrounds, folks from the North and South and East and West, married and unmarried people, kids and teens and adults and senior citizens, etc. According to I Corinthians 12, he expects us to not only work together, but to be exactly what the church needed.

I often wonder about the church members who don't attend any more. Didn't God expect them to be part of the stew? Are we missing an important spice because of them?

When someone dies or moves away, is the mixture ruined, or does God have a new recipe in mind?

I'm convinced that God has a way of making any recipe taste good.

*****

The Most Important Tool

The hammer was feeling mighty fine one day. He stood up tall on his handle and spoke in a big voice to the nail, "Hey, shrimp! I guess you know I'm the most important tool in the tool box. The carpenter used me all day yesterday. Show some respect! If you've got something to say to me, you'd better say 'Mr. Hammer' or I probably won't even answer you."

The nail, a bit surprised, decided the hammer was getting a little too big for his tool belt. "Oh, Mr. Hammer, your honor, your majesty and your so forth. It certainly does make one feel good to be used all day, doesn't it? I, too, am important, though. Without me, a house can't stay together. It's just a pile of lumber."

"Nail, you're nothing without me! You could only lie around, without me to drive you into the board," said the hammer.

"Without me, hammer, you could only tear things down," said the nail.

Just then, the carpenter came up. "Good morning, nail and hammer. Come get into the tool box, and please leave room for the saw, the drill, the chisel, the screwdriver and all the other tools. We're building a church, and I need all of you working together."

*****

No Food This Sunday

One of my pastor friends in a nearby church has had a persistent problem in his congregation. He said it looks like folks take turns coming to church. He may see a family for two weeks in a row, then invariably the third Sunday they'll be absent. Others come every other week. Some only miss once a month. Others come to church every Sunday, unless relatives are visiting.

Sounds like a food problem to me.

Personally, I've *got* to be in church every week, even on vacation. It's food for my soul. It's nourishment for my Christian life. Missing church, to me, is missing a spiritual meal. If people skipped meals as much as they skipped church, obesity would soon cease to be a problem in this country!

Tell you what: The next time your sinful nature tries to tempt you to miss church for little or no reason, promise yourself that you will not eat that Sunday. Simply decide that if you skip your spiritual food, you'll skip your physical food, too. That's only fair, right?

Either you'll be in church or you'll lose that weight you've been trying to shed for so long.

Seriously, friends, gathering together to worship God is a feast for our souls. Come every Sunday. Don't miss a meal!

*****

Love Your Family as Yourself

I was talking to one of the nicest men I know this week. I guess. He's always been gentle, kind and sweet. When the conversation turned to his church, though, suddenly he was mean and angry. It took me by surprise.

I understand that everything does not always go right, in any organization. We don't always agree with our boss. We don't always think our friends are doing the right thing or making the right choices. It's not all that unusual to hear strong opinions about others. Family is different, though. Any faults we find with our brothers or sisters or parents are usually kept within the family. Church is family.

Let's make it our practice to never speak harshly about our church family to outsiders. God has drawn us together to combine our varied personalities, skills, and gifts in service to God. He meant for us to be different. God uses our differences to reach a melting pot of a world.

See your church family through God's eyes. Take a second look at the faults you see in others, to find the benefit God meant for us through that particular quality.

Now we are the body of Christ.

*****

Summer Church

I can't change the world. It's too big.

I can't change summer, the season of vacations.

Still, there are two things I'd like to change about summer. It may be like "the voice of one crying in the wilderness," or like the sound of a tree falling in a deserted forest. Our lives are often transformed a little at a time, so I'll bring up these two ideas one more time.

First, when a person is far from home on vacation, Sunday is still Sunday, and God ought to be worshiped. God can be found wherever you are, and there are Christian churches wherever you are. Find one. Don't worry about wearing your best clothes, just find a place where you can join other Christians in worshiping God. Vacation is not taking a break from God.

Second, giving your tithes and offerings to the Lord should continue whether you are attending your local church or are out of town. Mail a check to your church before you leave. This is the faith community that supports you every day of the year. It's not a show or some type of entertainment that you only pay for when you get to attend.

These two ideas are dear to my heart. They are not popular, and I don't know that I've changed the way of thinking for many people over the years. Still, I'll continue to bring them up year after year.

*****

Let Them Serve

There are a lot of things that children and teens can do in the church, if we give them a chance. In fact, they often get excited about jobs that seem ordinary to many adults. It has been said that kids aren't the church of the future, they are part of the church now. Sounds good, but we still don't call on them to do very much.

Jesus had a lot to say about kids. He said to let them come to him, don't hold them back or block them in any way. He commended their kind of faith, trusting without reservation. We adults often seem hesitant to put our complete trust in God. We want to use our own ability until we find it inadequate.

Children and teens add a lot of life to a church. In fact, they would add even more life if we didn't insist on keeping them in check. We do our best to teach them that church is dull and boring, that excitement is out of place in worship. Why does church have to be dull and boring? Reverence can be exhibited in lively ways, too, can't it?

May your love of God be filled with excitement!

*****

Something from Nothing

My Great-Grandmother Fish was a quilter. Of course, she never bought fabric. Everything was made from scraps. Any old shirt, any sheet that got a hole in it, any dress the girls outgrew was fair game to be part of Grandma Fish's next quilt.

The untrained eye of a young boy couldn't see any way that a striped shirt, a linen dish towel, and a frilly dress could be part of the same quilt. They were too different. Grandma Fish had a way, though, of combining pieces of extravagantly different origins into a quilt of amazing charm. It was as if those pieces were meant to become available at precisely the same time.

God does that kind of work, too. He can weave the lives of incredibly different people together into a wonderful church, in a pattern never seen before and never to be duplicated. Can anyone say somebody new doesn't fit in? We need to work with the understanding that God's eyes see possibilities we cannot even imagine.

Praise God for each and every person. Did you think we were just scraps?

*****

Not Out. Otherwise Engaged.

I don't understand why some circumstances allow me to work more efficiently than others.

For instance, when I'm working on the final 'put it all together' part of a sermon, I can often do it better while driving down the interstate. All those key points need some kind of order, and interstate driving allows me to toss all the ideas into the air and have them fall into place. I'm driving along in my own little world, amidst constant motion.

Another place I've found that's good for putting a zillion ideas into proper order is the hospital waiting room. When you're awaiting the completion of a friend's surgery, it seems time stands still. You don't know exactly when the doctor will be finished, so you must try to forget about the clock. When you are not conscious of the passing minutes, it clears a space in your mind to toss around ideas, and it makes no difference how much chatter is going on around you. Sometimes I've done the equivalent of five hours of work in just one hour in this 'lost world.'

A coffee shop will sometimes work in the same way, but not always. A room in the house that I don't usually sit in does not seem to work. Somehow what I need is a 'safe place' or sanctuary in the midst of a lot of chatter or noise.

Wait. Maybe that's a clue. It's akin to how a church service is a sanctuary in the midst of a noisy world. It's a safe place to put the pieces of your life together.

There is something inside each of us that is looking for sanctuary.

*****

New Life Makes Me Tired

Your pastor is tired today, isn't he? It's the day after Easter.

It is a giant celebration, actually the most important day on a Christian's calendar. Sure, Thanksgiving is an important holiday, because people have to direct their thanks, and it's hard to ignore God. Christmas is even bigger---that baby in a manger is a sign that God keeps promises. Easter, though, is the promise fulfilled, of new life in Jesus Christ.

Maybe you are tired, too. We've concentrated through the many weeks of Lent on the cross and the love behind it. We've 'given up' things for Lent. We waved the palms on Palm Sunday, relived the betrayal of Maundy Thursday, and felt anything but good on Good Friday. Easter was Sunrise Service and Morning Worship, with maybe a breakfast feast in between.

Then the whole family gathered for a feast and hiding eggs and..... well, we're tired.

The rabbits and the chicks and the eggs of Easter are all signs of new life. The new life will come, after you rest up, but only the way a Sabbath can bring it: Recentering on God.

You've been reminded of the eternal life that only Christ can bring. Grab hold of Christ.

"Come unto me, all who are weary and heavy laden, and I will give you rest."

*****

Chapter Ten: Faith Sharing

Telling others about salvation through Jesus Christ is known by many different titles, including witnessing, evangelizing, leading others to Christ, and getting people saved. I like to call it faith sharing because that's how you get it: By faith. You can't reason someone into heaven or even buy their way.

Difficult News

It's hard to talk to people about Christ. I know it is. Some of the greatest evangelists still get nervous.

I think it has a lot to do with how different this news is. Sure, it's Good News that Jesus died to pay for our sins. It's not like our normal conversation, though. It's not like the weather, which we really can't do anything about. It's not like talking about politics, since most legislation is worked on far from where we live. The good news we long to share is life-changing, and life saving. It's more important and immediate than what we normally talk about.

To share the important, extremely relevant news about Jesus making a way for us to have eternal life, we need to establish a relationship with people. As the old saying goes, "People don't care what you know until they know that you care."

Maybe it's not the Good News that is difficult to share. Maybe we have trouble trusting others enough to share our lives with them.

*****

"Witness"

It wasn't even a good book, kind of simple and poorly written, actually. It was the writing on the bookmark that caught Rat's eye.

This had been a lousy week for Rat Turley, one of a lifetime of lousy weeks. Monday had been that nasty hangover, because his girlfriend moved out on Sunday, because he'd slapped her on Saturday. Tuesday and Wednesday had brought past due notices in the mail. Thursday had not been his day, and Friday wasn't looking too good, either.

The book, with the bookmark that caught Rat's eye, belonged to the new guy at the plant, something the guy had his nose in at lunch time. Rat didn't know who the guy was.

"For all have sinned, and fall short of the glory of God," it said. What kind of a bookmark was that? Yet it somehow spoke to Rat, spoke loud. Yeah, he fell short. He was always falling short. He was the poster child for the Fall Short Society.

Rat pulled the bookmark out of the book, and found that the bottom said, "If we will confess our sins, he who is faithful and true will forgive us our sin and cleanse us from all unrighteousness."

The guy came back, and Rat Turley just had to ask what all that stuff meant. And he was told.

And, to make a long story short, well, that's when the angels rejoiced.

*****

Church of the Wide Woods

The animals of the Wide Woods would get together each Sunday in the Clearing to worship God. The bears, the deer, the raccoons, the birds and all loved their fellow worshipers and wished that every animal in the Wide Woods could enjoy this worship time with them.

Some types of animals, though, were not represented in this "fellowship of the Clearing." No beaver had ever come, for instance, though they seemed like good, industrious, clean animals.

In the Clearing one Sunday, someone (I really don't know who) wondered aloud, "Why doesn't someone invite the beavers to be part of our group?"

But who ought to do it? Who had the most in common with the beavers? The deer? Surely not -- "The bears have similar fur." The bears? -- "They're more the size of the raccoons than we bears." The raccoons? Surely not -- "They don't live in trees like we do. Their homes are near that of the herons." The herons? "Surely most animals have more in common with beavers than does a wading bird."

Though none volunteered to invite the beavers to Sunday worship in the Clearing, they would have been welcomed had they come on their own.

One day, the beavers did come on Sunday to join in worshiping God in the Clearing. They were glad they came, for they were indeed welcomed and felt a real nearness to God and the other animals.

Someone (I really don't know who) asked the beavers what led them to join in the "fellowship of the Clearing."

"It was a rabbit," they said. "We were impressed that an animal so unlike us would go out of her way to extend a paw of friendship."

Let anyone who has an ear, listen to what the Spirit is saying to the churches.

*****

Walk-Ins Welcome

When was the last time you opened the door for somebody else?

Don't misunderstand me, now. I'm not talking about a door to a car, or to a room or to a building. I'm talking about the kind of door you can't see.

This week I was buying a few items at a grocery store in a big city. I was in the express line, with no one behind or in front of me. "Hello," the cashier said, smiling broadly. "Just another lousy day, I guess."

Now, I recognized a chance to mention our God. Was I scared? Sure, happens every time. Did I want to just keep it to myself? Sure, happens every time.

"No," I said. "God has really blessed us in a lot of ways." I was so proud I spoke.

Well, it was as if I was opening the door for this young lady.

And she walked right through it. "Really, that's true. God has done a lot for me lately." She smiled as if to say, "Hey! I witnessed to my faith! I actually did it!"

Sometimes when we include God, the most important part of our lives, in our conversations, it does more good than we planned. We may be giving someone else an opportunity to witness to their faith.

When is the last time you opened the door for somebody else?

*****

Knock, Knock. Who's There?

Opportunity knocks from time to time. It doesn't always ring the doorbell, though it's right there. It doesn't always knock on the right door, either. Sometimes opportunity just lightly taps on the window.

My goodness, if opportunity had the good sense to knock in the proper fashion, on the right door, when we were paying attention and ready to listen, and loud enough for anybody to recognize that it was indeed opportunity that was knocking , well, usually we'd open the door. Usually.

Instead, opportunity goes begging. It seems that those least likely to make full use of an opportunity are those that answer. What a shame.

I suppose it's the biggest shame when we're talking about an opportunity to reach others with the Good News of Jesus Christ. Evangelism is an opportunity to change lives, now and eternally. Perhaps we could see that it was opportunity, but thought someone else in the church (or some other church) would surely answer the door.

*****

Add One More Thing

It's just one of those months.

I can't help but stare at my calendar sometimes. It's absolutely too full. People aren't meant to live like this. This month is out to get me. With God's help, though, I know I'll get through it.

Still, my life is far from filled in another aspect. There's still plenty of room to share my faith. I don't do near as much of that as I want to.

There may not be room for even a few more things on my calendar, but you and I both need to learn how to make the most of opportunities to tell folks about the better way of living we've found through Jesus Christ. It's like adding salt to a full cup of water; though the cup seems full, you can stir more salt in, and somehow it fits.

Dare we ask God to work opportunities into our schedule? I've got to admit that there have been many times that God has done something similar. Someone I really needed to visit, but never found time for, suddenly appeared in my path at a store, or near me in the bleachers while watching a ball game. If given a chance, God will open doors and smooth paths.

"You are the salt of the earth."
*****

These Four Walls
The winds blow. The cold surrounds.

We stay within four walls.

Months pass.

The sun beats down. Bright skies

continue.

We stay within four walls.

When do we come out?

Not weather, not weather. Life's cold

keeps us in.

Life's sunshine keeps us in.

Is this abundant life?

Jesus calls for no walls.

Step out in faith.

There is much more.

The heavens are torn.

*****

It's Here Someplace

My favorite Bible has a green and tan cover. It's a New Revised Standard translation, and each page has references at the bottom to quotes or sermons from John Wesley, the founder of Methodism. It originally belonged to my wife; she found another she liked better and, knowing that I admired this particular Bible, she gave it to me.

Where is it?

I used it in the pulpit on Sunday mornings, every Sunday through June 7, and then it disappeared. I am absolutely certain it got packed when we moved. Nothing was anywhere in the house when we left.

Therefore, I know it's here someplace. We still have unpacked boxes in the attic, each carefully labeled, so it is certainly in a box that just needed one more item to fill it up, and I didn't think it was necessary to list that one item--- my favorite Bible.

Ever have that happen to you? You can't find your favorite this-or-that, and until you find it, your heart just seems out of rhythm.

That's often how people describe a human's need for God. There's something we need, and it feels like it must be our favorite thing, and nothing seems quite right until we find it. God completes us. God fills a void inside us that nothing else can fill.

Since I lost my favorite Bible, I've used another that has a lot of similarities to my favorite Bible. Still, life will be just a little off until I find it.

Help others find what is missing in their lives. Help them find Jesus.

*****

Bringing Light to Winter

I sure was glad to get past December 22, this year's shortest day. Each day now gets a couple minutes longer, from that short day of just under ten hours.

That's the toughest part of winter. The cold we can stand, with a little extra bundling up. It's the lack of sunshine that gets people down.

Consider this: There are some days when the average worker leaves for work in the dark, and returns home in the dark. Every hour of sunshine is spent at work!

Often in the winter, I end up walking my big dog, Alfie, after dark. It's rough! Even the best sidewalks have an occasional uneven place, and Alfie gets so perturbed at having to wait for me to get up off my face and brush off while he just stands beside me. Pick up your feet, man!

Jesus said, "Now, you are the light of the world." He meant that the Spirit of God in us should be shared with the rest of the world. It's so they don't stumble.

We all need a little more light.

*****

Flew the Coop

Did you ever want to cook something old-fashioned, just to see if you could do it?

Well, see, I had this bag of frozen mixed vegetables. I had a cooked chicken breast. I decided I'd try to make a chicken pie, like the ones some of those older ladies at church bring to the pot luck dinners.

I've been cooking for a long time. I even cooked at a couple restaurants in my younger years. We also own lots of cook books. I could do this.

I boiled the vegetables on the top of the stove. I made up a tasty gravy using chicken broth and mixed it with the vegetables. Then I made a thin biscuit dough and poured it on top.

Let me tell you, after I cooked it in the oven a little while, it looked great! Victory! Great ingredients, great finish!

So why is this chicken breast still sitting on the counter?

I made a chicken pie without the chicken.

To me, that's like living a wonderful life without God in it. The main ingredient is missing.

"In Him was life, and the life was the light of all people." John 1:4
*****

Chapter Eleven: Maintaining, Part Two

Without maintenance, even the best machine will eventual break down. For instance, the human body is considered by many to be the best machine ever made, and we know that it has to be constantly looked after. Your spiritual life has to be monitored constantly, to catch problems (hopefully) before they get out of hand.

Struck a Vain

Some don't quite understand why some of us are so picky about keeping the third of the Ten Commandments, "Don't take the name of the Lord in vain." It seems so harmless at times, as when we're startled and say, "Oh, God!," or when we're mildly surprised and say, "My God!" Wouldn't it bother you, if someone called out your own name, excitedly and with a raised voice, and when you came running, you'd find that they didn't really mean to bother you at all? And then they did it time and time again!

We know it is wrong to say things like "God damn you!", as if God were our slave and we could order Him to condemn someone else. It's certainly wrong to just say, "Jesus Christ!" as a strong word said in anger, without being in prayer at all. I would think it's just as bad to say, "God bless you," when somebody sneezes if you really don't care if God blesses them or not.

God's name is special and holy. God longs to hear us call His name, to speak to Him as friend to friend. It is a good and joyful thing to call out to God at any and all times. Don't cheapen His name by using it in vain.

*****

Life Stinks

Y'all don't remember this, but it happened.

Jonah got an assignment from God that he didn't like: "Go to Nineveh and prophesy against it." Jonah headed for the ends of the earth, trying to get out of God's focus. It didn't work! Jonah found himself in the sea, where a huge fish swallowed him (the part of the story people remember).

And that's when he started praising God. He was just thankful to be alive. He thought his life was over, that he would drown in the sea, but now he was inside a big, smelly fish instead.

Seems kind of strange, doesn't it? Can we praise God when the situation we are in stinks? Of course we should. We're alive one more day, able to interact with family and friends. We could look around *just a little bit* and see somebody whose situation stinks just a little bit more. We've got another chance to encourage somebody, or help another person head in the right direction.

It's very rare when we have a perfect day. It's very seldom that nothing goes wrong. In fact, most days could use a lot of improvement. Still, there's something good about every day. So, just like Jonah, when life stinks---praise God.

*****

Saving the Elf Shoes

One of my relatives was recently in a play. Part of his costume included a pair of green, pointy-toed 'elf shoes.' Somehow they got left with me, and when I told him, he insisted that he wanted them. "Don't throw them away!"

Now, to the uninformed, they look like something of little or no value. To him, though, they are a token of a great experience with a wonderful troupe of actors.

Do you have any elf shoes? I'll bet you have something in your attic or in a closet that is a memento of a special past event. Someone else might not see the value, but you do. Don't let anyone else clean out your closets!

I don't want to be saved in somebody's attic or closet(!!!), but I do want to live my life in such a way as to remind others of special past times of fellowship or shared learning experiences. Better yet, maybe something we do can remind others of God, in some small way.

"I thank my God every time I remember you, constantly praying with joy in every one of my prayers for all of you, because of your sharing in the gospel from the first day until now." Philippians 1:3-5.

*****

Throwing Out the Past

We save too much. We all do. As long as there is a place to store it, we keep it.

There are several categories of stuff we hold onto. Some stuff is saved because we might need it some day. Men, I think, are especially bad about keeping various nuts and bolts and screws; women are more into clothes and fabric, right?

We keep some things (and I agree with this) because they are occasionally useful. We spend years getting just the right tools or dishes, and though we don't use them regularly, at times they are just what we need.

Then there are the memories! We find ourselves holding onto children's crayon drawings, our marginally important certificates, newspapers with our names in them, Grandma's cook book. These are the most difficult things to sort through, or thin out, or throw out. They mark points in time. They are life event markers. They are physical representations of things written on our hearts.

In the Old Testament, people erected "standing stones" to mark places where significant historical events happened. When people would later happen upon these vertical rocks, they would search for someone who knew what event occurred at that location. The memory lived on.

That's similar to your grandchild asking, "Why do you keep this old, yellowed newspaper from 1971?" My grandma would reply, "To make little boys ask questions!"

*****

You Are God's Treasure

You are God's treasure, though all may not see it.
You give God pleasure, growing bit by bit.
Measure by measure, you're filling with
    God's Spirit.
Becoming more treasure as more Light you
    admit.

You break the mold, you come in backwards,
You conquer the wrong sins first.
You're farther along in the tougher battles,
But at the easy fights, you're worst.

Some other believers would turn you away,
Because of your obvious sins,
But I need you here, battling with me,
For in places I lose, you win.

We all have our weak spots, though none
    are the same.
We're all Christian babies. As sinners we
    came.
My strengths are not yours, and yours are not
    mine.
I accept you as brother, hooked to the same
    Vine.

*****

119

Commitment

Where do we learn the concept of commitment? It seems some folks are more inclined to be committed in all they do, while others seem to always be half-committed in any endeavor they engage in. I've been pondering this in relation to church attendance and membership.

Certainly family upbringing has a lot to do with commitment. If your parents were the type to never miss a Lions Club meeting, or Sunday school, or a day of work, I believe you'll be somewhat the same. Even without your parents talking to you about commitment, I think their example will influence your habits greatly.

Your views about honesty relate to commitment. If you don't mind fudging on your taxes, you won't mind telling your boss you were sick when you actually just needed a day for Christmas shopping. However, if you are scrupulously honest, you will be the kind that always keeps your word. And you'll remember that when you joined the church, you promised to support it with your prayers, your presence, your gifts and your service.   Your honesty makes you show up on Sunday.

Somehow God's commitment rubs off on us, though I don't understand it all yet. God keeps His word, He's honest, He's completely dependable. Those are things I build my faith on. God is committed to us, though historically humans have faltered in their commitment to Him.

I think I can see all around me that the more we're committed to God, the more committed, and honest, and dependable we are in all areas of our lives.

*****

It's Time for What?

It must be spring. Our horseshoes pitching club's season starts soon! I'm pretty excited!

What a broken road of sports participation I've traveled! As an adult, my first great love was volleyball, when my wife and I lived a couple years in the Philadelphia suburbs. When we moved to Georgia, I favored running and softball.

During my early ministry years, my son and I played a lot of basketball. I also played tennis for a couple hours every Monday morning.

For the past decade, I have loved basketball, although it is usually just 'solitaire,' shooting baskets by myself. I also spent time regularly on darts.

Now my biggest interest is horseshoes. No longer is it just flinging iron in the back yard; it has blossomed into league play and tournaments.

Remember Ecclesiastes 3:1? "To every thing there is a season, and a time to every purpose under heaven." I still miss softball at times, and I'm tempted also to run just one more 5K run sometime soon. This is the time for horseshoes, though, the right situation and the right friends.

Even in the church, there is a time for everything. Songs get replaced by newer ones, casual attire takes the place of "Sunday best," automatic withdrawal takes the place of offering envelopes.

God is the same yesterday, today, and forever. God was creative in the beginning, and God is still making life new every day.

Walking with God is never dull.

*****

God In Us

"The Word became flesh, and dwelt among us," John chapter one says. Jesus was with God from the beginning, and He was God. My mind finds it hard to think that through. What was it like to be with one who always did the right thing, always knew the right word to say, who never hesitated in making the right choice? Jesus always thought the best of others, and was compassionate when they failed.

Jesus was God among us, and yet He said He'd be with us always. Don't you see? God still dwells among us, inside us. That's even harder to get a handle on, because we are the body of Christ. We are the ones who are to bring out the best in others. We are the ones that know what God would have us do and say. We are able, in trusting the Spirit within us, to not hesitate in doing the right thing.

I pray we'll spend our lives trying to hear God's direction more clearly. Our lives must be living witnesses to the incredible love of God for everyone on this earth. As Jesus told Peter, "You hold the keys to heaven and hell."

We've got to keep the gate swinging open.

*****

Waves of Ministry

Ministry comes in waves, doesn't it?

We're all ministers, working for Christ in our own ways, once we've committed our lives to Him.

It just seems that at times we're up to our necks in ministering to others, maybe comforting the grieving, or helping somebody find their way to Jesus (takes a while sometimes), or serving the needy.

And then come times when there's not much going on. No problem plops itself down on our doorstep. At times when the waves aren't so high, we need to take the chance to check out where we are in our relationship to Christ.

You know, you can take your hands off the steering wheel sometimes on a straight stretch, and before you know it a curve comes up, and you're off the road. John 15:4 reminds us, "Abide in Me, and I in you. As the branch cannot bear fruit of itself, unless it abides in the vine, neither can you, unless you abide in me."

There are avenues of service opening up every day. Maybe this is a good time to reassess, to check on how well we're connected to Jesus, so that we'll be ready when the next big wave of opportunity to serve comes rolling in.

*****

What Is a Cold Day?

It feels cold today. Is that crazy? It was in the upper twenties one day this week, about twenty degrees warmer than in my hometown in New York State. How could I be cold?

I've actually been a Southerner now for thirty-nine years.. Any tolerance I have for cold weather is long gone, decades in the past.

Alfie, our dog, is the one who tolerates cold well. We're not exactly sure what breed he is, since he just showed up one day as a pup, but it seems obvious he is related to those sled dogs in the Arctic regions that sleep in snow drifts and consider it warm.

Last year, the temperature one night got down to sixteen degrees, and we packed pine straw (pine needles, for you non-southerners) around his dog house for extra insulation. He appreciated it! The next night it got down to eighteen, two degrees warmer, and he chose to sleep outside.

When you are of a warmer nature, the world seems a warmer place! Get it? Those with God's Spirit inside seem to find less to complain about. The world seems less cold.

*****

Chapter Twelve: Seasonal

Some of the improvements God makes on us are tied directly to a particular time of year. That's not to say there are seasons when God isn't working on us! One look at us, and God must say, "Ah, I see something else that needs an upgrade."

Lent Me What?

Well, I missed Mardi Gras again.

The name is French for "fat Tuesday," you know. It's the last day before the beginning of the church season of Lent, on Ash Wednesday.

Since Lent is traditionally a time of 'giving something up for Lent,' as a way of remembering Jesus' sacrificial death on the cross, Mardi Gras became popular as a sort of last fling before a period of deprivation.

Now, from my experience of going on many diets in the past, it would seem the worst thing you could do is have one final blowout before a time of strict discipline.

So I missed Mardi Gras again.

Until Easter, I'll be cutting out all those little snacks that have made me gain twenty pounds in the last two years. That's often how temptation works, isn't it? It's just a little sin, over days and months. Before we realize it, we've eased away from a close relationship with God.

So, every time I reach for that extra snack and stop, I'll remember that Jesus died for my sins. Even ones as simple as little snacks.

Have a blessed Lent. Remember the cross.

*****

Hope and the Woodchuck

I always look forward to Groundhog Day, February 2. I try to pay close attention as to whether or not that furry animal, which we called a woodchuck where I come from, sees his shadow on that special day.

The folk theory says that, if the groundhog sees his shadow that morning, winter will hang on another six weeks. If he doesn't see his shadow, spring is just around the corner; that is, it will be an early spring.

There are at least thirteen groundhogs in the U.S. and Canada that make it their business to predict the coming of spring! As you can imagine, they don't all agree.

Usually the predictions are split pretty evenly.

The two that get the most press, and the ones I give the most credence to, are Punxatawny Phil in Pennsylvania and General Beauregard Lee in Georgia. This year, they agreed: We'll have an early spring. Many people rejoiced.

Is there really a connection between woodchucks and the coming of spring? I doubt it. My favorite reference book, the Bible, says nothing about these animals predicting the weather.

*****

Easter!

Easter is a great day!

Think about some of those crazy symbols of Easter our culture has come up with, and don't be afraid to celebrate!

The Easter eggs are a sign of new life, celebrating Jesus' resurrection from death, which brought new life for us. It wasn't enough for Easter eggs to be their natural white or brown---this is a celebration! There ought to be a profusion of color. And it wasn't enough to just use the eggs hard-boiled, until they cracked; plastic Easter eggs let the celebration continue.

Rabbits have become a big Easter symbol. What other animal proliferates and brings new life like rabbits? I like the chocolate ones, for new life in Christ is *sweet*.

In line with that same theme, marshmallow rabbits and chicks ("peeps") are especially sweet. They may not be the best for your teeth, but, HEY, this is a great holiday---loosen up!

The egg hunts are great---seeking new life, right? And besides, Jesus was known for always seeking the lost (as we also should be known).

Not everyone knows these symbols of the holiday are deeply Christian. Share your information. Use every device you can to tell the good news of our risen Savor!

But it does say a lot about hope, and the human need for it. We need to have hope that better days are coming soon. Hope brings light to our days, affecting our emotions, our health, and our ability to think clearly.

"And now, O Lord, what do I wait for? My hope is in you." Psalm 39:7

*****

Advent Snow

Snow really goes with Christmas.

When I was growing up in Spencer, New York, we children really looked forward to snow. There were so many wonderful things to do outdoors when it snowed, like sledding, making snowmen and snow forts, and a zillion other things. We spent very little time thinking about the inconveniences for adults that snow caused, like slippery traveling to work or grocery stores, slippery walkways and freezing clothes on the clothesline.

Snow was especially important at Christmas, because many of our presents depended on it, such as new sleds. One of my favorite presents ever was a "flying saucer." This snow toy was about four feet across, circular and looked a bit like an inverted pot lid without the handle. To ride it, you carried it to the top of a hill and jumped on, holding tightly to the two burlap straps provided on the inside edge. It was *fast!* It also was oblivious to direction. It only knew to go downhill.

More importantly, snow is an insulating layer over dormant vegetation. In spring, when the snow melts, the grass and flowers spring forth in brilliant green and other colors, thankful for the blanket that brought them a springboard to new life.

Advent is kind of like that blanket of snow. We pause for a season to celebrate and remember. We put behind us grudges and prejudices and other problems.

Christmas will bring us new life.

*****

The Perfect Gift

Christmas comes sooner than you think. We look forward to it, yet it scares us to know there are only "___ shopping days left." There is a lot of pressure to get all our relatives, and a few others, the "perfect" gift.

The pressure may continue until every last gift is bought. It may last all the way to Christmas. Can you see why Christmas is more than some people can take?

Let me point you in a different direction.

Understand, once and for all, that there is only *one* perfect gift. In all our shopping, far and wide, it's easy to miss it, but we really know exactly what the perfect gift is, the one that will fit everyone on our list, the one that fits *us*.

The gift was given many years ago, and is still new today. God gave His Son. They called Him Jesus. Therein lies the joy of every Christmas. To know the satisfaction of sharing the Perfect Gift, you must first receive it yourself.

So give yourself a break, cut back on some of the pressure. You'll never find the perfect gift in a store; just buy one that sincerely shows your love. Join friends and family in experiencing again the wonder of Christmas, when God gives His Son that the world might be saved.

May the Gift be new to you again this year!

*****

Dark Christmas

The cruelest part of the Christmas story is found in Matthew 2:16-18. Herod had asked the Wise Men to report back to him when they found the newborn King, "so that he might worship Him," though more likely that he might do Him harm. The Wise Men are divinely directed to not go back the way they came; Herod is incensed when he realizes they are not bringing him the requested information. Herod orders every male child in Bethlehem killed, two years old or younger. The senseless tragedy casts a dark shadow over the miraculous birth of a Savior.

Christmas often has its dark side. People have heart attacks at Christmas time, sweethearts break up, loved ones die--- all in the midst of this earth's most joyous celebration. Darkness creeps in, even at times of abundant light.

Amazingly, light always wins. When darkness comes into the light, it never swallows it up. Rather, darkness is always dispelled.

"This is the message we have heard from Him and proclaim to you, that God is light and in Him there is no darkness at all." I John 1:5.

"What has come into being in Him was life, and the life was the light of all people." John 1:4.

May Jesus, the Light, dispel any darkness in your life.

*****

Too Late to Be Early

Every year, Christmas comes a little earlier for us.

So much goes on during Advent and Christmas, especially for those active in a church, that it's impossible to fit it all in. Most of the activities are inspirational and fun. Some are just plain mandatory! Even if you try to simplify, there is only so much you can cut out.

We love to decorate for the season. Those of you that helped us move to our present home are probably wondering about all those big gray tubs--- could all that really be Christmas trappings? Of course, not everything will be part of this year's decorating, since each house is different. It will take a lot of time to put everything up, maybe more than usual since nothing has a 'usual' place yet.

The calendar is filling up with dinners, special performances, and shopping days. We know we'll also need time for wrapping gifts and baking.

We start early because of the quiet part of Christmas. So often it gets left behind. We want to have an evening or two for driving around looking at Christmas lights. We want to have time to sit together on the sofa, drinking hot chocolate or cider and listening to Christmas music. We want to watch old Christmas movies on DVD's or even video tapes. We want time to take it all in.

Most all of us have heard the story of the first Christmas, about a baby born in a manger and visited by shepherds and wise men. Shouldn't we find some quiet moments, among the Christmas hustle and bustle, to think deeply about it?

*****

THE END

Made in the USA
Columbia, SC
09 April 2018